Captain Tom's
Life Lessons

By the same author
Tomorrow Will be a Good Day

Captain Tom's Life Lessons

Above All Be Kind

CAPTAIN SIR TOM MOORE

MICHAEL JOSEPH

MICHAEL JOSEPH

UK | USA | Canada | Ireland | Australia
India | New Zealand | South Africa

Michael Joseph is part of the Penguin Random House group of companies
whose addresses can be found at global.penguinrandomhouse.com

First published 2021
001

Copyright © Captain Sir Tom Moore, 2021
Illustrations copyright © Piers Sanford, 2021

The moral right of the author has been asserted

Page 63, Martin Luther King, Jr, from the 'Conquering Self-Centredness' sermon
delivered at Dexter Avenue Baptist church, 11 August 1957, permissions sought from
the Estate of Martin Luther King, Jr; page 127, Field Marshal Montgomery, *A History
of Warfare*, HarperCollins 1968 (page ref unknown); page 139, Ernest Hemingway,
A Farewell To Arms, Penguin Random House (page 226).

Every effort has been made to trace copyright holders and to obtain their
permission for the use of copyright material. The publisher apologizes for any
errors or omissions and would be grateful to be notified of any corrections that
should be incorporated in future editions of this book.

Set in 11.28/18.87 pt Stempel Garamond LT Pro
Typeset by Jouve (UK), Milton Keynes
Printed and bound in Great Britain by Clays Ltd, Elcograf S.p.A.

The authorized representative in the EEA is Penguin Random House Ireland,
Morrison Chambers, 32 Nassau Street, Dublin D02 YH68

A CIP catalogue record for this book is available from the British Library

ISBN: 978-0-241-50401-7

www.greenpenguin.co.uk

'I think my greatest ambition in life is to pass on to others what I know.'

Frank Sinatra (1915–98)

———————————

Publisher's Note

Captain Tom took one hundred years to write his first book. His next followed rather more quickly. Tom finished writing *Life Lessons* in December 2020, having devoted the same unflagging commitment to it as he had to his fundraising. Delivered the week before Christmas, the completion of *Life Lessons* capped a truly extraordinary year. Through the distress and tragedy of a global pandemic, this modest old soldier with a kind word for everyone became an unlikely but worthy talisman for the whole country. With his passing, the publication of *Life Lessons* has taken on a poignancy that Tom had never intended. And it's clear from the pages that follow that he had no fear of the end. While we can mourn his loss, we shouldn't feel sorry for Tom himself. He lived a good life and he made a difference. If Tom's final year was a gift that helped see us through difficult days, *Life Lessons* has the valedictory feel of a final farewell – a distillation of the wit, warmth and wisdom that made him so special. Perhaps it will help us all be a little more Captain Tom. For that, we can be truly grateful.

Contents

Prologue

*E*very morning, as I open my century-old eyes to another day of life, I lie in my bed and allow my body to catch up with my mind. Once I'm fully awake, I swivel my head on my pillow to check the time, hoping that it is past 6 a.m. but knowing that it's likely to be nearer 4 a.m., much to my dismay. I've never been a good sleeper and a decent night's rest has become something of a luxury.

No matter what the hour, I remain there for a while and ask myself, 'How am I going to feel today?' I wiggle my fingers and toes and wait for each muscle to respond. Some are stiff, others not so much. My right leg has been a nuisance since I fell at the age of ninety-eight, so I pray it will be a little less painful today.

Lying very still, I can feel my heart pounding inside its bony chassis. It's a miracle to me that this old fuel pump has been ticking over since 1920. Thanks to its unfaltering perseverance, yet another day has dawned that I've never seen before. It is certainly one that I will *never see again. This fact, alone, is enough to confirm to me that today will be a good day.*

Delighted by this thought, I swing my legs out of bed and pull myself to an upright position. Everything is done at a snail's pace and I sit for a time to let my system warm up. I'm not as steady on my feet as I used to be, so I have to wait a bit before shifting into first gear. Bending forward with care, I place my slippers on my size 11 feet and then sit back up to allow the delicate mechanisms to settle. A human body is much like an engine and you have to treat it with a certain amount of respect, especially when it's such a vintage model.

When I'm ready, I stand gingerly and – using my trusty walking frame – make my way into the bathroom. I am painfully aware that if I were to fall again, I could be reduced to a state of helplessness, as I was once before. At the very least I'd have to call out and wait for help. I don't plan to fall but nor do I want to be treated like a child.

Taking things slowly, I wash, dress and shave before going downstairs to make myself a cup of tea – milky, weak and sweet. My entire morning ritual takes me roughly an hour and has rarely varied in all my years. There's no hurry. I'm not on a time trial, after all, and patience is something I've acquired a great deal of lately. Once I've sifted through my morning mail, I settle to the newspaper that I read cover to cover, paying special attention to the obituaries, the contents of which alone can rescue a day. Other people's lives are usually so much more interesting than my own. Making a mental note of their ages, I must admit, however, to allowing myself a small smile if I've managed to outlive them. At my age, anything is worth celebrating.

Despite my physical limitations, I still greet every morning grateful to be alive. My grandchildren assure me that, even with people living longer these days, it's still pretty rare to be as old as I am – which they calculate as 100½. They've started measuring my life in half-years, as anything longer might be too optimistic. It might be quarterly soon. This makes me laugh because it reminds me of when they used to declare that they were 5½ or 6½ in order to appear a tiny bit older. There's small merit in my doing that now but I enjoy the idea of coming full circle.

No matter how many years or half-years I have spent on this Earth, the one thing I have learned is that it's important to start each day positively. By rising each morning and completing my few simple tasks with a small sense of pride, I introduce some structure and motivation to my day, whatever it may bring. My little routine might not suit everybody, but I could do a lot worse, and – nobody can deny – whatever I'm doing, it seems to be working for me.

I.

Eat Your Porridge

> '*Attitude is a little thing that
> makes a big difference.*'

Sir Winston Churchill (1874–1965)

———————————

Long before I was conscripted into the Army at the age of twenty in 1940 and had a sergeant major inspecting my uniform, the shine on my boots and the polish on my buttons, I was a tidy person who came from a tidy family. I was certainly never a 'lie-a-bed', and no Moore ever slouched around in casual clothes or left the house looking anything other than presentable. That just wasn't done, and the family ethos shaped my life.

Grandmother Hannah wafted through life in starched white cotton smelling of lavender and had not a hair out of place. Grandfather Thomas and my parents were just as meticulously dressed and never wore tatty clothes, so I followed their lead. As the newly conscripted 'Private T. Moore' I relished military discipline and was delighted to find myself under the command of an officer who shared the same high standards, insisting that we shave each morning, with or without hot water. There were to be no scruffy soldiers on his watch, so we were always well turned out, even in the most inhospitable conditions.

The days of being inspected are long gone but I still start each day with the intention of looking tidy. It pleases me when people comment on how well dressed I am and makes me feel better about myself. Looking our best isn't a question of money or class, but of setting our own personal code. It's down to each of us to make the most of ourselves and take care of the one small thing in life that's within our gift to control. For me, that usually involves wearing a crisp white shirt and a tie, clean dark trousers and a jacket if required. The idea of spending all day in my pyjamas or what I would call 'gardening clothes' has never been for me. It may feel like a comfort, but it is small change compared to the satisfaction and confidence that comes from making a little effort.

I would also never dream of leaving home without something in my stomach. Throughout my childhood I started and ended my days with Ovaltine, a hot drink made of cocoa powder and malt stirred into full-fat milk. This wholesome, high-protein fuel was especially important when I was roaming the Yorkshire moors with my dog Billy, often miles from anywhere and in all weathers, with food the last thing on my mind. It came as a huge shock to me when I discovered that Ovaltine wasn't provided as a matter of course in the British Army. On my first day in the cookhouse, I was given a cup of tea instead and that's been my hot drink of preference ever since. In truth, I sometimes don't know how I'd get through a day without it.

Porridge was the Moore family breakfast of choice and something I have stuck to with almost religious zeal. Rarely a day goes by when I don't eat my porridge. Even when I was deep in the jungles of the Far East, in unbelievable heat with every kind of biting insect hungry for the taste of Yorkshire blood, I asked the Army cooks to make my porridge just the way this Dalesman liked it.

When I were a lad, blowing on my oats and waiting for them to cool, I'd study the colourful cylindrical tin that I'd poured them from, fascinated by the man in a frock coat who dominated the label. I noted his black, wide-brimmed hat, his white lace collar, and the fact that the company was established in 1877, just forty years or so before I was born. In what would now be called a mission statement, the company declared that: '*Every mother knows there is no other cereal that can take its place as a food to build strong boys and girls.*' I can't argue with that.

Having a decent breakfast inside you may seem like a small and unimportant habit to develop, but it allows you to start as you mean to go on and head out into the world firing on all cylinders. Comrades of mine in India took to enjoying curry for breakfast but, as we say in the North Country, 'There's nowt so queer as folk.' That wasn't for me, but I don't see any reason why breakfast shouldn't contribute to life's rich tapestry.

Thanks, in part, to my nourishing start to the day, I've remained the same weight all my life, which has served me well. In generally fine fettle, I find myself free of diabetes, high cholesterol or unhealthy blood pressure, much to the amazement of the medical staff I come into contact with. 'Is that all?' they exclaim when they discover that the only pills that I take are painkillers for my leg. I smile and await their further expressions of surprise when they then find out how old I am.

I'm sure one of the reasons I'm so hale and hearty is that we only had natural, wholesome food when I were a growing lad. There were no supermarkets selling ready meals overladen with fat, sugar or salt, and no takeaways other than fish and chips. My childhood dinners of roast beef and Yorkshire pudding, sausage and mash or toad-in-the-hole were all homemade from produce bought directly from country folk. These traders sold their wares in the street from wooden carts laden with potatoes and onions, apples, strawberries, butter and eggs. Everything was locally grown, seasonal and freshly harvested, so there was nothing out of step or exotic.

Unpasteurized milk was delivered twice a day by a lady carrying a heavy pail balanced on a yoke across her shoulders and ladled out with a measure. Meat was bought from the butcher and there was plenty of it – ham and bacon, pork chops, lamb and beef. We used to say that the only thing we didn't eat on a pig was the squeak. There were no refrigerators, but we had a windowless pantry with a thick stone shelf that kept everything beautifully cool. From it, my mother selected the ingredients to make us three square meals a day.

Fortunate as I was never to have gone hungry as a child, I was still taught moderation in all things, so I was never a glutton and – later in life – I never smoked and I hardly ever drank alcohol. At family mealtimes, we were served just enough food so there was little or no waste. If out, I might have a 'penn'orth' of chips in a waxed paper cone from the chippy. I'd only ask for a larger portion with a fillet of fish if I were hungry – and I'd get the lot for the princely sum of sixpence. By contrast, when I look at the size of portions today, I'm often staggered. People are served vast mounds of chips and a piece of fish as big as a whale, hanging over the plate edges by several inches. No wonder there are no cod left in the sea.

Another thing that helped keep me fit and well throughout my life was that I never stopped moving from virtually the day I learned to walk. If I wasn't out rambling or walking the dog, I was cycling or – later – motorcycling, and I didn't ever sit still for long, even in adulthood. There was never a specific regime to follow, but by moving my body daily I developed the habit naturally so that a day without exercise was as rare as it was unwelcome.

I realize now how lucky I was to grow up where and when I did, but I try not to memorialize the past as 'the good old days' because I think that's largely a myth. My parents and grandparents would probably have called them the 'bad old days', because theirs was an era of wars and workhouses, mass unemployment and social injustice. Water had to be boiled if wanted hot and, for many, there were no inside toilets. People suffered from all kinds of terrible diseases that doctors hadn't found cures for yet, there was no NHS to help, and society endured a great deal of inequality. But there were still good days amongst the bad days, just as there have always been. It's called Life.

We are undoubtedly living in happier times with improved living conditions, far more opportunities for employment, better healthcare, greater access to information, and the kind of state support that was never around for the underprivileged in my day. Groundbreaking human rights laws have been brought in to protect us from harm and there is a far better structure to policing and government. As a natural-born optimist, I see the future as brighter still and have every confidence in the youth of today. I'm especially envious of the exciting years that lie ahead of them, waiting to be explored. I firmly believe that the current generation will lead us to a better world in which people are kinder to each other, less selfish and care far more deeply for our environment.

At the same time, blessed with so much more freedom and opportunity to express their individuality, I hope they don't lose sight of the importance of a certain amount of discipline and order in their daily lives, along with the value of living a balanced life and beginning each day in a positive frame of mind, with the intention of doing some good. My advice to them – and to us all – is to eat your porridge (or your breakfast of choice), dress the part, think kindly of others and take care of yourself. All of these will reflect well on you and do a great deal for your own self-esteem.

If we are happy about ourselves – and I have found that the smallest things can give me a boost – then others will be happy with us too. In leading by example, our actions will be like dropping a pebble into a pool of water and rippling goodness out into the world. That is surely the best way to start any day.

2.

The World is Your Oyster

*'A journey of a thousand miles starts
with a single step.'*

Lao Tzu

———————————

One of the nicest things that happened to me after my 2020 'Walk with Tom' was that I was made an honorary colonel of the Army Foundation College in Harrogate, Yorkshire. At the end of the first long lockdown, I was invited there to inspect some three hundred junior soldiers who had recently graduated.

Having walked up and down the rows of immaculately turned-out men and women, I was asked to say a few words. Smiling kindly, I told them, 'You are setting out on a future of unlimited scope. The world is an oyster, and it is yours to open. Don't follow the crowd. Make your own way. Keep looking ahead because that's where the future lies, and it is there that you will find the chance to improve your own lives and those of others, as well as changing your perspective.'

I meant every word and hope that each of them has enough get-up-and-go to investigate their surroundings and take advantage of the many opportunities that come their way. They mustn't waste a moment, but they must also be prepared to do their part in supporting others and helping those less fortunate. Mainly, I hope they try to see the best in everyone and treat others as they'd like to be treated – something I have always tried to do.

We only have one spin around the circuit, so it's important to enjoy a wide range of experiences and see and learn as much as we can in the time we're allotted. Travel especially keeps our minds alive and our bodies active. It also makes us humbly aware of our own good fortune. Exploring new worlds and experiences, either in person or through the medium of new technology, encourages us to ask questions of others and ourselves, even if it may not always bring us the answers we seek.

The overgrown track is always the more interesting option than the well-trodden path, and if the idea of that frightens us a bit, then all the better.

I grew up in the 1920s in a small rural community where people rarely even went to the next village. Few had cars so they travelled only as far as they could walk. The first time I ever left Yorkshire as a young lad, it was to visit London. My strongest memory is how crowded, busy and noisy the capital was, teeming with people and cars, along with horses and carts, bicycles, double-decker buses, taxis, hansom cabs and hundreds of trading vessels plying up and down the River Thames. To put it in perspective, London had a population of around eight million, while Keighley's was in the low thousands, so the difference seemed astounding. I felt overwhelmed and excited all at once, and the things I saw certainly broadened my horizons. While my trips out of Yorkshire after that remained rare, it didn't put an end to my wanderlust.

Although I'd had a sheltered childhood, I was always interested in maps and yearned to see more of the world. At eighteen, I was taken to Switzerland just as the prospect of war was beginning to loom over Europe. Accompanied by a favourite uncle, I travelled by steam train, boat and ferry to what felt like a distant land. In Lucerne, I found myself surrounded by people who spoke a different language, ate different food, had different opinions and politics, and even dressed differently. It made me appreciate that the way I had lived up until that point wasn't necessarily the only way. Nor was difference anything to be scared of. In fact, quite the opposite. By seeking out other worlds, we introduce variety into our thoughts which prevents us from getting stuck in one place or with one viewpoint.

It is generally a lot easier to jump on a plane nowadays, but we don't even need to do that to see the world today. If we can't escape physically, then the beauty of modern life is that we can still travel in our minds, which is where the Internet, radio, television and literature are invaluable. Most of these cost little and, if you are a member of a library, then books and films can be free. I've always enjoyed reading as a way of opening a window on the world, but lately I've been so busy that I have a stack of books to catch up on.

These are mostly biographies of other people's lives or something about history, although war stories have never appealed much because I have to confess to flicking through the pages and thinking rather cheekily, 'Been there, done that.' Instead I focus on books that have some resonance with life today.

Having lived through a global conflict and thirteen changes of prime minister, I am keenly aware of the importance of paying attention to world events and staying both fully informed and connected. I was eleven years old when we had our first house telephone in 1931, and I was as fascinated by this staggering innovation as kids are today by their smartphones. After a GPO engineer installed the brand-new apparatus in our hallway, we stood there as a family staring at it for a while, not sure what to expect. The first time it rang we almost jumped out of our skins, so unaccustomed were we to the noise.

To make a call, we had to wind up a handle that rang a bell in the local telephone exchange. We then told an operator the number we'd like, and she (always a lady) attempted to put us through; a process which often took considerable time. Eventually we might be connected to a jangly voice at the other end – not nearly as clear as calls are now. I embraced the technology as a boy, but many older people were afraid of the 'new-fangled' machine in case it bit them (or – worse – cost them a few farthings). I recognize that tendency in myself a bit now and try to remain receptive to modern developments.

These days young people are so competent with new technology that their ability astounds me. At the swipe of a finger or click of a mouse, they can summon up a virtual tour of anywhere from York Minster to the temples of the Far East. In seconds, they can locate a clip of some ancient television programme I mentioned in passing or show me remarkable footage of some of the battles I took part in during the war. They can download apps that play games and teach them new skills, create music or turn them into cinematographers. They can practise yoga, speak Italian, or read a book whose pages turn as if by magic. Thanks to the wonders of the worldwide web, the proverbial 'oyster' has suddenly become a lot easier to open.

Few of the current generation can comprehend how much the next big innovative change in my lifetime altered things in ways I could never have imagined. The advent of television in the 1950s was a game changer even though there was only one channel to begin with, provided by the British Broadcasting Corporation on whom we had previously only relied for wireless radio transmissions. The first of these, incidentally, happened in 1920 – the year of my birth.

As televisual technology improved and other channels such as Granada emerged, we were astonished to discover that, without moving from our front parlours, we could watch anything from the Queen's Coronation at Westminster Abbey to a youthful David Attenborough in some of the world's most exotic and difficult locations helping zoologists capture birds and other wildlife to take back to London Zoo. The few programmes that were on offer all ended at the same time each night with a white dot on a black screen and a continuous high-pitched tone to remind us to turn the set off.

Television still provides an invaluable lifeline,

especially for news, and ensures that when I'm talking to people these days I can generally keep up. But armchair travel is no substitute for first-hand experience, and I don't like to think that my roaming days are over, as there's always something new to see and do. Luckily for me, every day still brings surprises and last year I had one of the nicest invitations of my life.

Having mentioned almost in passing during a television interview that I'd quite like to go to Barbados one day, I was flown there to feel the sun on my old bones, watch some cricket and meet a group of fellow centenarians. This wasn't something I ever expected to be doing for my hundredth Christmas and New Year, so it was a real treat. My youngest daughter Hannah and her family accompanied me to make sure I got there safely and didn't get into too much trouble.

While folks today are far more accustomed to flying around the world than I ever was, I'm still careful not to take this easy access for granted and to remember to savour all that I see and experience. I've tried to do that throughout my life and, now that I'm on my final few laps, I make an even greater effort to do so.

Relishing each new experience is important in our everyday lives too. Home or abroad, I often see people sitting around, not moving about much, or doing owt productive. Instead, they're heads down in their phones and having fewer and fewer conversations, which I worry has the potential to make their world smaller or less interesting. This physical inactivity has been especially true since the pandemic, with people being forced to work from home and converse via online meetings; something that I hope doesn't become too commonplace. We may have made great progress in communications, but in doing so we can also risk losing something.

It would be a tragedy if human beings only ever spoke to each other through devices because nothing can replace the wonder of personal interaction. Engaging with strangers or going to work and building a rapport with colleagues is a kind of adventure all by itself. If we don't get that kind of first-hand experience, then we can miss out. When talking with somebody while looking them directly in the eye, we can see their expressions, watch their gestures and pick up the tone of what they're saying – little of which can be gathered remotely. Only with such direct contact can we understand their true feelings and be more open to what they're really saying. This kind of one-to-one connection allows us a glimpse into the inner worlds of others, and in doing so expands our own.

Don't get me wrong. I am not a Luddite and I'm not against change, not by a long chalk. After all, I've experienced more than most in my lifetime. Even though tasks that once seemed relatively simple – like thumbing through a dictionary or getting up to turn on the telly – now seem more complicated in many ways, I still do my best to keep up. Every day I count my blessings that I live with teenage grandchildren who are almost always on hand to assist, because – thanks to them – I'm probably more switched on than many of my vintage. I don't pretend to be an expert, but I now own a smartphone and a tablet and, unlikely as it sounds, I'm familiar with social media, live TV links and even video conferencing, which has opened up the rest of the planet to me. Who'd have thought it?

The happy truth is that we humans are incredibly adaptable and generally respond to new experiences and challenges with courage and an admirable resilience. Even my grandparents, who were at first rather shaken by the sound of somebody's voice down the end of a telephone line, eventually got used to it and found the courage to use the apparatus themselves. When embracing new experiences, we should always be mindful of those for whom life can feel as if it's changing too far and too fast. For some, too much choice can be overwhelming, and they're tempted to give up before they've begun. All too quickly, they can be locked out of the goings-on in the wider world, and not just when they're home alone. Nobody uses a cheque book any more and even cash has fallen out of favour, so people won't be able to manage if they aren't able to use a computer or order everything with a single click. For them, the world is only going to shrink.

As I first discovered in my teens, we don't live in a bubble at all. There's a great big universe out there of people and machines, of joy and suffering, of politics, exotic foods and strange, wonderful and sometimes curious cultures. By remaining eager to experience it all, we can better appreciate our own place in society and decide upon the contributions we might be able to make.

Looking beyond the pandemic, there has never been an easier time to explore the wider world, or even our inner worlds. As I told the Harrogate graduates, it's important to stay curious and to strive for a better understanding of the challenges faced by those starting out on life's journey. But this is a two-way street. The older we get, the better placed we are to offer what wisdom and advice we can to those who ask for it. We can do this by sharing stories of our own adventures and mistakes. With luck and an open mind, others will realize the value of talking to someone who's had a life well lived.

Remember that the world remains an oyster no matter what age we are, and – although it may not always occur to those around us at first – one of the shiniest pearls that others might discover and come to treasure in it, is you.

3.

Be Comfortable in
Your Own Skin

'Live as if you were to die tomorrow.
Learn as if you were to live forever.'

Mahatma Gandhi (1869–1948)

———————————

There are some people who simply don't know what to do with themselves once they retire and relinquish the routines of a working life. This is especially true if they are also widowed or divorced and find themselves living alone, or far from loved ones. Left to their own devices, they discover that their own company often isn't enough. I suspect this is because they've never taken the time or had the opportunity to find out what they enjoy and can't imagine how to amuse themselves.

Instead, they sit disengaged, hoping that someone might call and cheer them up. Unable to draw on their own sense of self, this can lead to a spiral of decline which fosters a further loss of confidence that renders them unable to initiate something for themselves. As horizons narrow with age, it's unlikely to occur to them that by going out, helping someone, joining a group or calling up a friend they'll enjoy the surprise of where that might lead them. Men are especially bad at this because they're generally not as good as women at opening up about their feelings or telling people how lonely or unhappy they are. They think they're not meant to show weakness, so they often bottle things up and fester about them, which can be extremely detrimental to mental health.

An inability to make peace with your own company can become even more of a problem by the time you get to be as old as I am. As age claims increasing numbers of your nearest and dearest, you'll likely be spending a great deal of time alone with your thoughts. This is why it's important to try to learn how to entertain yourself and be comfortable in your skin early on. Of course, being on your own isn't merely age-related. There are plenty of people who find themselves isolated from the rest of the world for all kinds of reasons (including an unforeseen pandemic), so unless the skills to manage that are nurtured then life can become difficult and distressing.

One of the best things about being in lockdown was that the sense of being confined to barracks against our will made us all appreciate the benefits of being outside in the fresh air. It encouraged the (permitted) exploration of local parks and heaths, of rivers, beaches and lakes, and of walking, cycling and swimming, all of which are not only good for the health but can be done alone and without costing a penny. Being surrounded by Nature has always been such a tonic for me, and it certainly beats sitting inside feeling glum. I was fortunate to understand the value of this as a lad.

Family circumstances meant that I learned to be self-sufficient at a young age and never to depend on conversation or instruction from others. Because of this, I was perfectly happy to wander the moors alone for days at a time, go for solo bike rides, and – later on – to make my own way in the armed forces and in business. I couldn't have had a nicer father in Wilfred Moore, but he lived in a world of silence due to his profound deafness, so normal conversation wasn't possible. Most of our communication was done through signs and gestures and we learned to work companionably alongside each other without sound. And because I couldn't bombard him with questions all the time, I had to figure things out for myself. This is how, aged twelve, I fixed my first motorbike (bought for half a crown) and only showed my father when it was restored to full working condition. No one helped me; they just assumed I'd manage it and I did. I was always allowed to be who I wanted to be.

Thanks to a strong sense of contentment, I was also never short of things to keep myself happily occupied. Once I saw how dependent my father was on my mother for all his food, washing and personal needs (as was the norm for his generation), I was determined that I would be different. Aside from the fact that this meant I learned how to cook as a boy – and still prepare all my own meals – I've always been able to find something to do whether it be baking a cake, going for a walk, reading a book, watching a favourite Western or getting on with the housework.

My mother may have been a traditional Yorkshire housewife of her era, but she was bright and very forward-thinking. She raised me to understand that chores were chores, regardless of gender. I was regarded as just another pair of hands in the kitchen and was happy to help. Under her watchful eye, I became what people these days might call a 'new man', and there's no shame in that. My favourite uncle, Arthur, was a first-class baker and pastry chef so he was an additional role model for me.

By the time I was married for a second time and had small children, I was the only chap doing the ironing or taking the family washing to the launderette, but it never bothered me what other people thought about that – or anything else. What did I care? I was equally happy to do the weekend cooking, the pot washing or the vacuuming and never confined myself to the traditional male household tasks of mowing the lawn or tending to the car. As soon as my two daughters Lucy and Hannah were old enough, they were similarly enlisted for whatever job was required, even if that meant gardening, building a chicken coop or sliding under the car to change the oil. I taught them the importance of navigational skills and they could do everything from changing a light bulb to wielding a hedge trimmer. My goal was that they'd be fully equipped for the future and ready to take on the world by their teens, but also to find pleasure in their own company and have pride in achieving the little things in life.

As a widower in my eighties and nineties, I was still on my feet puttering about all day because there was always something to tick off my daily 'to do' list. I might go into the garage and work on the car or tidy the shelves. I'd head up into the attic to see what I could throw out, maybe do a bit more in the garden, cook something or take a trip to the supermarket. Once I had a folding bicycle, I'd take it and the family dog to the Kent marshes where we'd travel for miles.

With modern technology bringing together far-flung communities and offering online courses and activities, even those less physically able (and, increasingly, I must include myself in this group) can pursue new interests or old enthusiasms unhindered by geography or self-consciousness. Never be afraid to take the first step or to break out on your own.

I appreciate that being completely comfortable with yourself isn't always so easy for young people growing up in an environment that encourages them to seek the constant approval of others, especially through social media. And while I wholeheartedly applaud the way they have embraced technology – and am grateful for how much they've taught me – I do worry that those already lacking in self-esteem might sometimes be looking for it in the wrong place. It's important that we instil in children the confidence to make up their own minds, have the courage of their own convictions, and not measure their self-worth through what others do or think. Only then will they learn to appreciate their own company.

I was never a hanger-on or a show-off when I were young. I tried to be authentic to my true self and didn't feel that I had to join in with friends, especially if they were being reckless. This was never more the case than when I saw how daft they were after supping too much beer – and how badly out of pocket. Devoted as I was to my motorbike and the freedom it gave me to ride out on my own, I knew that if I wanted to keep my machine, I couldn't afford to waste what few pennies I had on ale. It mithers me to see some go out drinking for hours on end, desperate to do as others do rather than fear they're missing out. But I understand the lure of that, too, and have to confess that I've not been entirely immune to this temptation myself.

I was only ever inebriated once in my life, though, on a trip to Kashmir during the war when I had too much brandy in order to impress a lass. It was gormless of me to forget that the men in my family had little or no resistance to alcohol, and I paid the price the following day with my first – and last – hangover. My head hurt, I was sick to my stomach, and felt absolutely rotten. Never again. Anyone who survives that experience and then repeats it only has themselves to blame. It's important to have some respect for your body and to remember that it is the only vehicle you'll ever have to carry you down the road.

If folk are lacking in self-confidence or feel dissatisfied with what they have then that can also help fuel the modern-day urge to compare themselves to others. Instead of being perfectly content with what they have and happy for the success of those around them, people can often convince themselves that the grass is greener and become envious of those they fear are ahead of them in the race. Sadly, so many of those they aspire to emulate are celebrities or those who offer a lifestyle far beyond their reach and completely unattainable, which only leads to further resentment.

I can't think of a single time in my life when I begrudged anyone for having a better lifestyle, job, house, partner, body or car. I may have aspired to a more powerful motorbike once or twice, but I was never jealous to the point of unhappiness because I knew that what I had was right for me and was also comfortably within my means. Instead, I found my pleasure in enjoying what I had, not what I hadn't.

Contentment is highly underrated and stems from being comfortable with who we are, grateful for what we have achieved, and not comparing ourselves to others. That is a fast lane to discontent. Happily, age can help with this too, as money and material possessions no longer feel like such important indicators of our status in life once we are older. All that earnest striving for an improvement to our circumstances and saving up for nice things starts to fall away with time.

When I were a lad, if someone asked me what I wanted to be when I grew up, I'd make them laugh by replying: 'A millionaire.' It wasn't a serious ambition and I never did manage it, of course, but as I helped raise almost £40 million for the NHS you could argue that I achieved my dream forty times over, in the end. And I am beyond wealth in the richness of the life I'm living now, fulfilled and content.

One interesting feature of old age is that time becomes the sole currency and the only thing that matters is how we feel about ourselves – and how others feel about us. All those possessions we've surrounded ourselves with no longer seem so crucial to our place in the world, and we realize that we've accumulated far too much stuff.

Another surprising pleasure of the passing of the years is letting things go, as there is very little that we need but we realize there are items that others might like. A long time ago – it must have been ten years since – I invited my girls to help themselves to whatever they wanted from my house, telling them, 'Take it now. Don't wait 'til I'm gone. I don't need any of it.' I'd much rather they appreciated these so-called heirlooms while I was still alive.

Now whenever I'm asked, 'What would you like for your birthday, Tom?' I am always at a loss. It's the same at Christmas. 'A new leg?' I might suggest, with a wry smile. Truly, that is all I want for. The only thing that matters is the people I keep around me and the happiness of those I love.

If you're at ease with yourself and what you have then it also brings valuable perspective when it comes to listening to the advice and opinions of others. Being satisfied with my lot taught me to know my own mind and to trust my own judgement. Drawing on my self-belief and self-sufficiency, I was happy to ride solo and make up my own mind about which road to take.

This has helped me through all kinds of difficult situations. From an early age, with my father unable to hear and my mother and sister in their own little world, I was able to find solace in the solitude and silence of the moors, a place where I was the most content. Dressing myself appropriately in a tweed jacket and cap, proper walking shoes, thick socks and a woollen jumper, I was never caught out by the weather because I knew how to read the signs. Nor did I ever get lost or stuck out overnight, because I knew the place like the back of my hand and had the confidence to trust my own instincts.

I had a few good friends and – eventually – managed to get by with a few girls all right, but unlike many of my friends I chose not to commit myself until I was much older. Once war broke out, I made a deliberate decision to remain unattached emotionally in order to save the lass's suffering – and my own.

During my unhappy first marriage when I had no home life to speak of, it was vitally important that I be fully self-reliant because I needed to find ways to keep my mind and body occupied. I loved my wife, in spite of everything, but I longed for time to myself. That's when I took up motorbike trials because it was something positive and different and it rekindled some of my happiest days on the road. Once again, I found myself outdoors on my own in the one place where I could think freely. Aside from my father, none of the men in my family had married well and I convinced myself for a while that I'd brought that loveless relationship upon myself. It sometimes felt as if it was only what I deserved and payback for the carefree years I'd enjoyed before.

In time and on my own reckoning, I realized that I'd just been unlucky, and, to my relief, it all worked out perfectly in the end. Before too long, I was married again with two lovely girls. Over the years I hope that I have also taught them the importance of being equally at ease in their own skin and I think I may have succeeded, because I'm happy to say that they are forceful, independent women with their own – often strong – opinions, who have each made a success of their home and working lives. Nothing could have made me more proud than to see them confidently forging their own paths through life. And I am certain of one thing – they will never be boring or bored.

4.

Keep Smiling Through

'There is always something we can be concerned about. The secret is to rise above it and do whatever we can to make the world a better place.'

Dame Vera Lynn (1917–2020)

————————————

Dame Vera Lynn sang it so well and her words have resonated with me since I first met her in the jungles of Burma in 1944. The lyrics of her most popular number, 'We'll Meet Again', are all about remaining hopeful that tomorrow will be a good day, and that blue skies will drive the dark clouds away. A very special lady, she died at the age of 103 just after I started my walk, but not before she'd sent me a message congratulating me and wishing me luck. Movingly, her letter arrived on 18 June 2020, the day she left us. I will always treasure it.

Like her, I've always been a happy little soul and never one to complain or feel sorry for myself. I wasn't brought up to be miserable and realized early on that complaining never solved anything. Instead, I've always tried to find a little bit of joy in every day, no matter how small. When I was younger that came from having a beloved dog, growing up in the countryside and watching the colours of the moors changing with the seasons. In later life it was the joy of hearing my girls' laughter or the beauty of a summer's day. Now it can be something as simple as a nice cup of tea, a good night's sleep, a life-enhancing obituary or a slice of Victoria sponge.

I've also tried to retain a healthy sense of humour, even if it is sometimes so peculiarly dry that people don't always get it. I certainly inherited my sunny outlook from my family, and it has served me well. My parents were an unassuming couple without a mean bone in their bodies, and whenever I was facing something difficult my father used to promise me that things would be better in the morning. My Granny Fanny was a similarly cheery person with never a cruel remark. With all three of them, gratitude played a big part in their cheerful nature. They may have been virtually teetotal, but their glass was always half-full.

I have adopted the same approach throughout my life and have much to be thankful for, even now. I am mostly grateful that I'm still alive and still have my mental faculties, especially after what I witnessed my second wife Pamela endure towards the end of her life. There are so many people worse off than me, and whenever I go to hospital for any reason, I look around and think, 'Flippin 'eck, what cause do I have to make any complaint?'

And whilst I am deeply appreciative that I've been able to maintain such a high level of independence, especially during the repeated lockdowns of the pandemic, I was doubly thankful that I wasn't so self-reliant that I was stuck somewhere on my own.

If my family hadn't been on hand to care for me, I'd probably have spent the last few years in a nursing home, where I mightn't have lasted as long as I have. I wouldn't have been downhearted, though; I'd have found something to cheer myself up, probably by helping out the staff and chatting to them, just as I did at the nursing home where Pamela spent her final years. After all, nobody objects to the squeeze of a hand or a smile. You might even get a smile back and if you do, then just think of the good you've done by transforming someone's downcast face into a grin.

I'm also grateful that I live somewhere with easy access to fresh air and green spaces. When I think of the thousands trapped inside for months on end, especially the elderly and infirm – as well as the people who are called upon to care for them – I count my blessings twice. I worry for them and for all who suffer from depression and other mental health issues who must feel so utterly cut off from the world. There's no one to smile at them or help lift their spirits, and that is a crying shame.

None of us is immune to sadness, of course, and there have been times in my life when I was laid extremely low by events. These included the suicide of my beloved uncle Billy, the collapse of my family building firm, the ending of my first marriage, and Pamela's degenerative brain disorder.

Whenever bad things happen, though, I refuse to think, 'Poor me.' Instead, I remind myself that nothing is permanent. This can be a tremendously comforting thought to hold on to, especially when the going gets tough. All things must pass, as they say.

My personal dramas are petty in relation to terrible world events and I always remind myself that I've survived worse. Life changes in all kinds of unexpected ways, so – filtering out the worry and fear – I focus instead on my unlimited supply of happier recollections from Yorkshire, my years in India during the war, or family holidays to cheer myself up. I have quite a good memory and can picture myself at any given time in the ten decades that I have thus far survived. Having watched my father hoot with laughter at Doodles the clown in the Blackpool Tower Circus each year, it's no surprise that I grew up to love clowns too. The mere thought of my father's infectious chuckle in anticipation of some dastardly trick Doodles was about to play on the Ringmaster can bring tears of joy to my eyes.

In these welcome visitations from the past, random reflections float in and out of my mind perfectly pleasantly. Travelling back through time, I can see myself as a little boy out with my father on the fells. I remember him watching me proudly when I found a bird's nest, the home of a long-tailed tit, and carefully showed him one of the eggs. Or I can see myself in my school shorts picking daffodils with my mother and sister Freda or having picnics with the whole family up on the high moors. Mine was an idyllic childhood immersed in the natural world and the mere thought of those days is enough to lift my heart.

Ever since I was small, I learned that there's always a bright side to a bad event if you look hard enough for it. The best example of this by far for me is the immense good that has come out of my fall. That was the biggest surprise of all, because tripping and breaking my hip in 2018 almost did for me and marked the beginning of what will become my inevitable end.

Yet, if I hadn't tripped over my feet that day then I wouldn't have needed to set out on my little therapeutic walk at all. And if I hadn't managed that, then none of the remarkable events that followed would have occurred. Instead, millions of pounds were raised for NHS charities which in turn seemed to boost the spirits of the nation and all because I was unlucky enough to take a tumble. As a bonus, I even managed to put Keighley and Marston Moretaine firmly on the map!

People tell me that there's going to be a film about me soon because of everything that happened, but I can't seriously believe that anyone would be willing to pay good money to see it.

If the filmmakers decide to go ahead, they'll have to think on it as they'll need different people to play me at different ages – preferably with kind smiles and ideally from Yorkshire so that they speak the dialect. Sir Patrick Stewart is from Mirfield but, at eighty, he's probably too young. And it can't be Sir Ian McKellen, who is eighty-one, because he's from Lancashire and, although I'm not quite old enough to recall the War of the Roses, the wounds still run deep. Whoever it is, I'll be tickled to think that I'm inadvertently giving work to a fellow OAP.

Fantasy casting aside, it amuses me that what

seemed like the worst day of my life when I fell accidentally led me to some of my happiest and most surprising years. It's astounding to me that I had to wait until the age of ninety-nine for life to become so extraordinary. Just when I thought that this lad born into 'God's own country' was biding his time in 'God's own waiting room', with not that much to look forward to, this incredible thing occurred. And not just to me, but to everyone.

People assure me that I am now a household name and, so far, I'm not too displeased about that. Best of all, wave after wave of goodness has emanated from my impromptu fundraising that keep washing back over me in ways I could never have imagined. Whoever would have thought that little Tommy Moore would one day be knighted, become an honorary Doctor of Science, and have the freedom of the City of Keighley? My father and grandfather would have laughed their socks off.

So, although it may often seem difficult to find any positives in a negative situation, and especially from all the hardship caused by the coronavirus, they can often be found in unexpected places. In a year that the world wanted to forget, there have been many unforgettable moments for so many, and not just me. Those who hardly knew their neighbours suddenly found themselves standing on their doorsteps each week clapping for the carers, singing, playing musical instruments or getting to know strangers across the street. Faced with the possibility of no income, no employment and little social interaction, thousands discovered their own humanity and did what they could to help others. They raised money for hard-pressed charities, provided comforts for frontline support staff, or shopped and cared for all those like me who were shielding.

As a nation, we helped each other through as one by one we discovered an inner strength we didn't even know we had. It is good to remind ourselves every now and again that babies were still being born and that the majority of people that caught the virus survived. There was even a benefit to the environment, as planes were grounded and the roads emptied of traffic. Air pollution dropped so massively that thousands of lives have likely been saved.

On a smaller scale, people discovered all kinds of stimulating experiences that could be enjoyed on their doorsteps. Bike sales surged as men, women and children took to two wheels and improved their general health. New companies emerged from the ashes of the old and many sectors discovered or invented different, innovative ways to keep afloat. I firmly believe that we will all emerge from these viral times to find ourselves living in a better world because of the outstanding, life-changing consequences of people's effort to be positive. Even with multiple and often unforeseen setbacks, we need to keep smiling through and continue to count our blessings every day.

When forced to focus on the important things in life, millions around the world discovered what we of a certain age have often taken a lifetime to find out – that all that really matters are the people who make you smile. None of us know what's around the corner and it might just be something magnificent. As I have discovered in my long life, things usually turn out all right in the end.

5.

Walk in Someone Else's Shoes

'An individual has not started living until he can rise above the narrow confines of his individualistic concerns to the broader concerns of all humanity.'

Martin Luther King, Jr (1929–68)

When I were a lad out roaming the moors with my dog Billy, it was the country way to knock on the door of a remote farmhouse to make sure that the occupants were well or see if they needed a helping hand.

This is because people living on the fringes of a community are often extremely isolated and might not see a soul for weeks on end. If they become muddle-headed, too old to cope, or are struggling financially, then it's always beneficial for someone to drop by. The very fact that a stranger knocked might make that day different to the day before and the one after, and that alone might end up making them feel a little bit brighter.

There was one poor farm way out on the edge of Riddlesden that was inhabited by an old couple who were both quite infirm. They only kept a few sheep, and it was clear that they didn't have much to live on at all. There was never anyone else around and no mention of family, so they just had each other to rely on. In spite of this, or perhaps because of it, they were always delighted to see me and would invariably invite me in to give me (and Billy) a little something to slake our thirst.

If ever they offered us something to eat, I'd generally turn them down for fear of depriving them, but sometimes they'd insist. One day they made me a sandwich as a special treat, but as soon as I took a bite into the bread I realized that the meat filling was off. Sitting at their kitchen table as they stood there smiling down on me, I didn't want to embarrass them so I did the only thing I could – I gobbled up the rancid sandwich with fake delight and thanked them most sincerely.

I never forgot that old couple and often wondered how they were faring. Years later, when I became one of the youngest members of the Keighley Rotary Club, I mentioned them to the charitable organizations we worked with so that they could check and see if some improvement could be made to their lives. After we opened a day centre for the disabled and lonely, I arranged for a volunteer driver to collect them so that they could be brought into town for a hot meal and to socialize with others for the day. It gave me such pleasure to see them there eating heartily and thoroughly enjoying themselves.

Mine was a small gesture, born out of a glimpse into their situation and a desire to help. By trying to walk in their shoes I realized that there were a few small but simple ways that I could make life a bit easier for them. It didn't cost me owt, but it seemed to mean so much to them and I was happy in the knowledge that I'd maybe done a little bit of good. Kindness is like that. It surprises you because you always get more back than you give.

I've seen first-hand how a little kindness and compassion can make all the difference to people from all walks of life and on different stages of their journey. It's something that's free for everyone to give and should be given freely. Thoughtfulness and humanity were core values in my family, so I was raised from the earliest age to show respect for others and be considerate of their feelings.

Grandfather Thomas, the original 'Tom Moore', was the greatest exponent of that. He came from nothing and had very little schooling, but he became a pillar of the community. Unusually, he made a point of paying not his men but their wives each week, as he knew that the wages might otherwise be wasted on beer and their bairns would go hungry. This thoughtfulness taught me a lesson in trying to see things from another viewpoint.

One of the causes that has become closest to my heart and which I hope my grandfather would approve of, is my wish to help those who are feeling lonely. From my own personal experience, I am bitterly aware of the misery of loneliness. I experienced it when Pamela first went into a home and I found myself living alone. Loneliness was already a national epidemic before the devastation of coronavirus, but the pandemic further isolated people of all ages and from all walks of life.

All those everyday things we take for granted – like young people playing with their friends, teenagers enjoying new relationships, or those just starting out at university – have been affected. The single, divorced and widowed, the reclusive and elderly are trapped and helpless to some degree. I worry about the impact this kind of forced isolation may have on mental health and well-being.

Since my walk, I have been lucky enough to be given the opportunity to promote some of my pet causes as part of the work of my foundation and happily, one of the projects I was invited to take part in directly addresses the problem of loneliness. Age UK has found that in a typical week more than two and a half million people aged over sixty-five talk to only a handful of people. Shockingly, almost a quarter of a million often go a whole week without speaking to a single soul. To try to address this, they came up with the 'Donate Your Words' scheme that encourages people to start a conversation with a pensioner. This feels both important and timely because it's also about walking in someone else's shoes.

Having felt the pain of isolation for ourselves, many of us have come to better understand the plight of those who are on their own, and the value of dropping by to say hello or offering a few words of encouragement to brighten their day. This is especially true for the elderly.

To promote the Donate Your Words campaign, I hosted my first podcast called *The Originals*, so named because we pensioners are truly the originals. This shone a light on how many amazing stories are waiting to be told, if only we take the time to listen. I may be biased, but I think it's fair to say that you name it, we OAPs have done it, so it's important to encourage the older generation to speak up. The lovely thing is that we no longer feel so old when we're talking about the past.

On my podcast, I interviewed some delightful men and women including a seventy-nine-year-old lady called Rose who'd kissed Elvis Presley, and a ninety-year-old man called John who'd completed fifty-two marathons in his lifetime and only stopped running at the age of eighty-eight. Then there was Winston, an eighty-three-year-old body builder who was still doing a workout three days a week in his own gym, and Rajinder who has been skipping with a rope almost every day for seventy years. There are so many other incredible tales stored in older memories that are like mine, full to the brim, so you never know what might pour out.

Too often, those who encounter the elderly only ever ask the same questions repeatedly, and in a tone usually reserved for children: *'How are we feeling today? Did we sleep well? What would we like for lunch? Are we warm enough?'* The answers to those are usually something like: *Fine, No, Nothing, Never.* But there's a veritable treasure trove of stories to be excavated if only people start digging, So, why not quiz us about where we travelled in our lifetimes or ask us questions that spark a conversation.

People are often amazed, for example, that I flew all the way home from India in a flying boat with a famous lady comedienne, or that I once appeared on a television quiz show called *Blankety Blank* hosted by Terry Wogan. They're surprised to learn that I frequently enjoyed the company of a beautiful Anglo-Indian lady in Bombay, or that I emigrated to warmer climes for a while after I finally retired. If you ask us about the most dangerous, risqué or surprising things we ever did, or which was our happiest decade, I promise you'll be in for a treat. And don't forget to quiz us on what lessons we might consider imparting to the younger generation.

I always love it when people ask me what life was like when I were a lad especially, because I so enjoy seeing their astonishment as I walk them back in time in my country boots. Few can fathom how different things were in a world that no longer exists. There's so much I can tell them, often using words and phrases that they've never even heard of; expressions that are now on the endangered list. Few young people know what a 'milliner' or a 'cobbler' is these days and find it hard to contemplate that people once wouldn't have dreamt of stepping out of their front door without a hat and gloves. Children can't imagine what it was like without electricity, central heating or gas. Or with no proper loos – more often than not just an outside lavvy or a chamber pot under the bed. Kids today throw their dirty clothes in the laundry basket without a second thought and haven't a clue what I'm talking about when I speak of a mangle with wooden rollers and a washing dolly known as a posser. The more I see the puzzlement on their faces, the more I realize that history dies with the person who is telling it.

It amuses me somewhat to think that if someone had spotted me in the street a few years ago, they wouldn't have given me a second glance. They certainly wouldn't know that I held the rank of captain or anything else interesting about my life. Yet I'm still the same person. Nothing has changed inside, except that because of all the fuss that's been made I am no longer as invisible as I used to be, and as so many old folks still are. That has really made people think, and wish that they'd asked more questions of their own parents and grandparents while they were still alive. Hopefully, it will also make the younger generation look at the old folks they know with fresh eyes and wonder what stories their own lips might tell.

Nowadays when people are out and about their heads are often elsewhere – sandwiched between headphones or face down in a telephone. You say hello and they look up in surprise and reply, 'What?' noticing you there for the first time. Yet taking the time to talk, to ask and to listen is a wonderful way to see somebody else's perspective and might just help to combat the heartbreak of loneliness or depression for many.

So many people are afraid of exposing themselves to something unknown or that they might not understand. Instead of being open to seeing life from another viewpoint, they'll put their heads down and hurry past.

I have found though that if I smile and say, 'How do?' then – after their initial shock – strangers of all stripes usually open up and often turn out to be lovely and friendly. But you'll never know that unless you stop and take the time to find out. So I try never to judge a book by its cover. I have had some of my most interesting encounters with the most unlikely of people by simply imagining what they might be feeling or thinking and then engaging with them.

We are all of us only wanting to connect in some way, so it's helpful to take a breath, think of others' needs as well as your own, smile, and see what happens.

Kindness costs nowt.

6.

Keep an Open Mind

> *'Men are not prisoners of fate, but*
> *only prisoners of their minds.'*

Franklin D. Roosevelt (1882–1945)

———————

My life has often felt like a series of events that have happened beyond my control. Instead of being overwhelmed, I've tried to face each new twist and turn with an open mind and, step by step, they have always led me somewhere new.

I suppose it's fair to say that, because of this, I am an opportunist: if I'm offered a chance, I'll jump at it. Whenever a challenge presents itself, I think, 'Say yes, Tom, and then work out how to do it.' Being spontaneous is one of the things that has kept me so young at heart.

This is because I think about life as grabbing hold

of every new opportunity and running with it. You never know what might happen or who you might meet. Being open to possibilities as they come to you has the potential to make every day so much more interesting. This is a lesson we can learn too late, often long after we have dug ourselves into a rut of our own creation. The rut can relate to the daily routines we adhere to (and I am certainly guilty of that these days), but it can also relate to our attitudes and opinions about everything from work to people, preventing us from being flexible and receptive to new adventures.

Look what happened to me during the war. Out in India I was about to be given my own tank to command in the ongoing battle for Burma but when my commanding officer discovered that I knew a bit about motorbikes he switched me to training up dispatch riders instead. Instead of wallowing in my disappointment and dwelling on what could have been, I welcomed the opportunity to work with bikes again and relished the chance to bring out the full potential of men who were often completely unfamiliar with mechanics and therefore at a disadvantage to their British counterparts. That experience led me to tank training and an early return to England – a move that probably saved my life.

Being open to chances in this way means that nothing has to be off limits. If you're out of work and want a job, then why not take any job – if there's one to be had – and see where it leads you? Once you've found yourself a position, you'll be better placed to find yourself another. And the next time you go for an interview, your prospective employer will be impressed that you were willing to take on any role.

I know this from my own experience as well as that of others. I went from a man who'd been something in the armed forces and in business to someone on the lowest rung of the ladder with no support at home or from anyone else. But I was open to anything that would keep me occupied, pay me a weekly wage and point me in the right direction. I never once doubted that I could make something new and improved out of my unhappy circumstances. Perhaps most importantly of all, I knew that if I didn't at least try I would always regret not doing so. I broke rocks in a quarry as a labourer and then became a door-to-door salesman for *Woman's Own* magazine, would you believe? But in both cases I tried to do the job to the best of my abilities.

I signed up for a correspondence course in salesmanship. I dressed the part, studied diligently, was never late and worked hard, but I was too soft-hearted to be a salesman, and so never quite able to seal the deal. In the end I accepted my commercial shortcomings and quit. Taking that initial leap of faith, however, inadvertently led me to the job that introduced me to Pamela and – ultimately – to more business success than I could ever have imagined.

If a door opens up, walk through it. If your path diverts you to somewhere new, embrace it. Nobody promised that life would be a clean, straight stretch of road. There will always be twists and turns, unexpected bumps and potholes and you never know where a diversion might end up. But it is the not knowing that is often the best part. Just believe in yourself, put your head down and follow your instincts.

We can learn a lot from children when it comes to instincts because they have so few inhibitions and are open to anything. If they see something interesting, they'll run to explore it. If a question bubbles up in their mind, they'll ask it. They'll also talk to anyone, even if it might be complete gobbledygook. My childhood friend Brian Booth used to say, 'There is no bad beer, just good and better,' and I think that the same may be true with children. There are only good ones and better ones because they haven't yet picked up any bad habits, prejudices or fears, so their spontaneity and enthusiasm are infectious.

Although human beings are incredibly adaptable, the older we get the more we can lose that sense of childlike wonder and can start to fear changes rather than remaining receptive to them. And if we're not sure of something, we're often afraid to show our ignorance by asking a question. Nobody will judge us for having an enquiring mind so we mustn't be shy or scared. If ever I'm in a confusing situation I will readily admit, 'I'm sorry, I don't understand. What do you mean? Please explain.' The fact that we're open to learning more about something unknown to us will always impress. This is another reason why it's important to surround ourselves with younger people as we grow older, for their youthful exuberance will freshly inspire and motivate us. Plus, when you've lived as long as I have, there's only the younger generation left to ask.

After my first marriage ended, I had two choices. I could dwell on the mistakes of the past or I could move on and be open to whatever life brought me next. Instead of licking my wounds and spurning all thoughts of another relationship, I allowed myself to fall in love again very quickly. Pamela made me as happy as a pig in muck, especially when I became a father for the first time as I was fast approaching fifty. Never once did I regret being a dad or think that I was too old for such a radical change in my life.

Having children so late put me in a position that few of my contemporaries shared. While they were enjoying being child-free and contemplating the prospect of grandchildren, I found myself surrounded by much younger offspring – my own and their friends. In my middle age (and it really was the middle, as it turned out), I had to stay on my game – doing school runs, attending sports days and taking part in all kinds of child-related events. It opened up a whole new world of younger people to me so that in my late sixties, heading towards seventy, I found myself swamped by teenagers, which was quite the experience and definitely kept me on my toes.

This is how we evolve; one generation open to learning from the previous one. It was the same with me and my parents, who I often thought of as old-fashioned. For example, when I think back to my father plonking away on the piano, I remember how out of date the songs seemed to me. Then along came music that I loved, the songs of Bing Crosby, Frank Sinatra, Tony Bennett (still singing in his nineties), which – in turn – seem obsolete to my grandchildren.

The songs they listen to now are completely foreign to me, but every now and again there'll be a part I like that sounds a bit like something I've enjoyed before. And so the cycle continues. I may know nothing about modern artists but I have been alerted to one or two including Stormzy, whose charitable donations I've been told about. I have to confess that I have no idea what his music sounds like, but any young man who donates £10 million of his own money to improving people's lives seems admirable to me. Those topping the charts today may have tastes a million miles from mine, but that doesn't mean to say I can't be open to what they stand for and maybe learn a little something from what they have to say.

We should all remember that we haven't learned everything and that we can still aspire to becoming better people, no matter how old we are. Even at 100½ there are opportunities to discover new things every day and I look forward to taking note of the information and engaging with it. Nothing learned through trying is ever wasted, and we are never too old to try more. Things change and they will go on changing, so if we close ourselves off and get stuck in a mindset, we will never change with them.

Stay informed, seek the opinions of others, especially those younger than you. Engage in conversations and debates. Accept new challenges. Keep your heart open and your mind fine-tuned at all times. It is never too late.

To prove the point, I've recently been asked if I'd be

interested in doing a charity skydiving jump. People tell me I'd be strapped to an instructor and pushed out of a plane at 10,000 feet to hurtle through the air at approximately 120 mph. Now, I have to admit that would be quite a thrill for this speed freak, and the experience would transport me right back to my childhood and the daring aeronauts who hurled themselves from hot air balloons floating high above the Keighley Gala.

Although I haven't committed to doing a skydive, I haven't said No either. The idea is sound enough, and I note that the current world record holder is 103. So, watch this space. My view is and always has been, 'Why not?' And, you know, that's not a bad maxim for life.

7.

Fortune Favours the Brave

> *'Moral courage is higher and a rarer virtue than physical courage.'*

Viscount William Slim (1891–1970)

———————

*V*irtutis Fortuna Comes or Fortune Favours the Brave is the motto of my regiment, the Duke of Wellington's, and its message has proved itself to be true time and again in my life, and not just in the war. Fear is something each of us will face in our lifetimes, and to survive it we need to be brave.

The most interesting thing about courage is that you don't know if you have any until you're required to call upon it. This is because no one volunteers to be brave; it is something that is thrown on you. And bravery doesn't only mean riding through the Burmese jungle knowing that the Japanese are a bullet away, as

I had to do with alarming frequency. Finding the courage to rise above your fear and either realize your goal or maintain some personal standard is something we frequently encounter, and it often brings the greatest rewards.

I have only been called upon to be physically courageous once or twice in my life, and I admit to having felt some trepidation, but I don't remember being terrified. It was far harder to be brave in my personal life, like the moment I decided to end my first marriage after so many years of sorrow. We all make mistakes, but there comes a time when we need to be brave enough to take responsibility for them and act accordingly. It is far better to be in control of our lives than to be a victim, and sometimes it's important to know when to let things go and walk away. Probably the bravest thing I ever did after that relationship broke down was to get married again, but that turned out to be the best thing also.

Years later, when I was in my mid-seventies, I had to find the nerve to organize a management buy-out of my company, a very stressful period that almost broke me. It was up to me, and me alone, to keep the promises I'd made to our investors and staff. I also needed to protect my family, whose home I'd mortgaged to pull off the deal. I am happy to say that I didn't lose my nerve and it all worked out OK in the end, especially once I figured out how to channel my fear of failure into the drive to succeed.

Later still, I had to be the bravest of all when the decision came to put Pamela into a nursing home. Having struggled to look after her for many years, I eventually accepted that I simply couldn't do it any more. I was in my eighties by then and her dementia meant that she could no longer be left alone so I just couldn't cope. Although I was desperately worried that I'd let her down, I visited her every day for the last four years of her life and eventually came to appreciate that it was the right decision for us both.

If, as I do, you continually strive to believe that tomorrow will be a good day then you likely won't give in to your fears. When something bad happens, I only hope that the sense of distress or worry about it will pass or at least lessen on the morrow, and it very often does. The future has a habit of taking care of itself. And yet, as human beings, we often can't help but worry about what might be round the corner.

If ever we are anxious or fearful of the future, it can be helpful to try to figure out what it is that we're really afraid of. Is it that we might be harmed physically, or damaged psychologically? Do we fear that somebody might threaten, belittle or embarrass us? If so, it could be worth asking ourselves if there might be another, more productive way to respond. When my daughters were little and did something rash like climb too high up a tree, their mother would get into a blind panic and beg them to come down, while I'd casually suggest that the girls take a pruning saw with them next time and make themselves useful. Rather than making them anxious, my unflappable confidence in them increased their chances of a safe descent.

In taking this approach, I must have inherited my dear mother Isabel's outlook, because when I was five years old I apparently went missing and was eventually found on a nearby building site where my grandfather's labourers were working. The men discovered me halfway up a tall ladder, sitting on a rung facing out. Terrified that I might tumble and break bones, one of the workmen ran to fetch Mother who returned to the site, looked up at my precarious position and called out gently, 'Come down now, our Tom. Your lunch is ready.'

Completely unfazed, I stood up, turned around and clambered down the steps to safety. It is often the calmness and courage of those around us that can help us make the right decision.

Never more so than during the war. Winston Churchill, Field Marshal Bernard Montgomery and my commanding officer in Burma, Field Marshal Bill Slim, all inspired me with their physical and moral courage. I never met any of them personally, but their leadership was magnificent.

'Monty' fought in the First World War and was shot in the lung. He survived and went on to have a legendary career as a British commander, dying a hero at the age of eighty-eight, as famous for his care of the troops under his command as for his victories in battle. Similarly, 'Slim' fought in the First World War and was wounded three times. Undaunted, he accepted command of the Burma Corps in the Second World War and stuck to his guns, despite a lot of opposition, to turn the tide of the war in the East.

Winston Churchill was much the same and refused to give up. A former army officer who served on the Western Front, he warned of the danger from Hitler even as Prime Minister Neville Chamberlain was advocating appeasement. When Churchill eventually took over at Downing Street, he led us through the greatest challenge our country had ever faced. Under his able leadership and with his stirring speeches, he united the nation in a way that few can understand today.

The truth is that people often need to feel led. And we need leaders to do that. Most of us don't need to use our heads for anything other than a hat-stand much of the time, so if someone comes along who exudes courage and confidence, we are encouraged to follow suit, or at least to try.

Courage can come in all shapes and sizes, however, and not all of my heroes are military. At home, my own father faced his disability with fortitude. So too did my mother, at a time when being married to a deaf man was anything but a soft option. While in my youth, my heroes were the fearless motorcycle riders of the Isle of Man TT races. Later on, a young woman inspired me through her presence alone. In 1944, Vera Lynn came to entertain us troops in the jungle, along with so many other selfless singers, comedians and musical artists.

If she'd been captured, the Japanese would have had a field day boasting of taking someone so beloved by the British. The very fact that she was there amongst us was enough to quell our own feelings of fear. How could we be afraid when this lovely creature had volunteered to be flown halfway across the world and into the jaws of death, just to make us smile?

These motivating figures of my youth inspired me to try to emulate them throughout my long life. Heroes and role models remain just as important to the young today, especially when they are able to use their position to change the world for the better. There can be no better recent example of this than the England footballer Marcus Rashford. I so admired this twenty-something's campaign against child homelessness and food poverty, lent weight by his own childhood experiences, and I was delighted to meet him at last year's Pride of Britain Awards.

And, of course, I can hardly fail to mention those tireless and heroic doctors, nurses, paramedics and care workers who put on PPE every day and push through their own fear of catching coronavirus to help those who need them most. Nothing in their training could have prepared them for what they've been expected to do, but they have been magnificent.

It was because I was so moved by their devotion to duty while in mortal danger from an invisible enemy, that I decided to see if I could raise some money in support. It was such a small thing to do by comparison; I simply moved my legs just enough to walk up and down my own garden. The only risk it involved was that I might fall again and do myself some more damage. Or that I would have to give up after a few laps and lose face very publicly. But I was determined that neither of those things would happen and ploughed on regardless, never letting anyone know that I was genuinely afraid I might not be able to finish. How could I have done otherwise?

Remember, everything is a risk. Life itself is a risk. We none of us know what will happen from one minute to the next. I was in danger the moment I was born during the tail end of the Spanish flu epidemic and I'm in mortal danger now, keenly aware that the odds are stacked against me. But I like to think I have the gumption to go on a bit longer, which is a word little used these days. Very often you need gumption to follow your gut feelings about something and, even if an endeavour ends badly, be grateful that you will always learn something from the experience.

One thing we learned from coronavirus was not to give up. We appreciated the value of standing side by side, metaphorically speaking, to get through the toughest times and raise each others' spirits. People plucked up the courage to do things they never thought they'd do. They retrained, took up new hobbies, reached out to strangers, set themselves difficult tasks to raise money for those in need and found strength within themselves to keep going, despite the outlook.

To me, that is as brave as anything I did, and I tip my hat to you all.

8.

With Hope in Your Heart

'May your choices reflect your hopes,
not your fears.'

Nelson Mandela (1918–2013)

———————

When I first visited Robben Island in South Africa, I was so moved to think that Nelson Mandela, the anti-apartheid campaigner who became the country's first black president, was imprisoned there for eighteen years, living in a tiny cell and sleeping on a straw mat.

I could only imagine what it must have been like to have been held in that forbidding place for so long. During his imprisonment, Mandela was poorly treated, lost his mother and son, and suffered from multiple ailments. He gave his life to his beliefs, but instead of giving up hope, he spoke only of peace and reconciliation upon his release from jail and continued to promote this approach until his death at the age of ninety-five.

People are defined by how they deal with life's unfairness, and not losing hope is key to that. It takes strength to start all over again, but you can make yourself believe that things will be better if you do. After the fall that nearly killed me, I became disabled overnight. It was over a year before I felt anything like my old self but, even then, I resigned myself to always walking with a frame. I reluctantly sold my car which sat idle in the driveway, accepting my place in someone else's passenger seat forever more. The loss of independence nearly crushed my spirit.

Ever hopeful that my leg would stop hurting one day and I might be able to get back on the mower or travel wherever I chose, I decided to focus on what I could still do and not on what I was no longer able to. I knew that – compared to those who were paralysed, bed-bound, or otherwise incapacitated – I was extremely fortunate. In eternal hope, I bought a variety of fitness machines to improve my mobility, along with a new bed and special cushions. I also started doing exercises and physiotherapy to help alleviate the pain.

I've been a believer in hope all my life as I think it is closely related to optimism, but with a specific goal in mind. It goes hand in hand with perseverance and resilience, and these three are often what hold us together. It is important not to lose our hope even if life doesn't seem fair or it feels simpler to quit. Giving up never makes things easier, and often makes things worse. There are several times in my life when I had to cling on to hope in testing times, but I managed it. I wasn't raised to give up.

The more I think about it, the more I realize that my hope probably comes from some sort of spiritual belief. I never claimed to be a religious person but deep down I may well be, because faith plays such a big part in hope. That was certainly true of my Granny Fanny, who I've always thought is watching over me. A devout woman with a strong spiritual life, she believed in God to the last. It was undoubtedly her faith that gave her hope, because if there was a God then all would be well and – as a good Christian woman – she'd be assured of her place at His table.

I attended her Primitive Methodist church to please her as a lad, and I also went to a regular Methodist church to appease my parents. To confuse my young soul still further, I donned a surplice and sang in a Church of England choir, so what does that make me? Broad church, I suppose. Perhaps I believe in them all.

A lot of people take great comfort in their faith and I still have hope that there might be a Heaven where I'll be reunited with my dear old father and my dogs, long dead. My true idea of Heaven would be riding an old pre-1950 Scott motorcycle around the fells on a glorious summer's day. I'd go up beyond Bolton Abbey on to Blubberhouses Moor and then further still. The air up there is fresher than any I know and the views at 1,300 feet take your breath away.

I haven't yet turned back to God in hope, as many seem to do towards the end of their lives. I think I'm still waiting to be convinced, as the bible always felt to me like a series of fables told by a good storyteller in order to sell a moral idea. There was one story that did stick with me from Sunday school, however, and that was the tale of the Good Samaritan who rescued the Jewish man he found beaten and robbed on the road to Jericho. A priest and a rabbi had previously ignored the poor fellow, yet the Samaritan whose people were often at odds with the Jews did all he could to help and even paid for the victim's care out of his own pocket.

The story may be a Christian one, but the moral at the heart of it has universal appeal, because if you follow its example then you cannot help but be a good person. I like to think that it is based on truth as it has such a strong message of compassion, mercy and hope in humanity. Heaven may be a grand idea but I'd like to keep my options open, so while I try to have a bit of faith in what comes next, I will live my life with a lot of hope, and a good dose of charity.

Faith doesn't always have to be spiritual or religious either. It can be a belief in your own ability and potential, or in the principle of right versus wrong, good against evil. You might have faith in those around you to love and support you, whatever you do. Or faith that the children you have brought into the world will go forward with your message of goodwill and optimism to help make everything right. I've been incredibly fortunate to experience first-hand how hope can transform all our lives in the most extraordinary way. And I was little prepared for it.

When people first began to take an interest in my walk, they told me that what I was doing gave them a little faith in the future and spread a bit of hope when times were so tough. I thanked them but I didn't really believe it until the money started pouring in, along with the thousands and thousands of cards and letters full of good wishes. That was astonishing to me, and it still is. I still find it hard to grasp how my effort, among so many, seemed to inspire such a display of national unity in which everyone was being so thoughtful and kind.

Aside from going to Windsor Castle to be knighted by my beloved Queen, I'd hardly left the house since lockdown began in the March, as I'd been kept in a protective bubble for so long. Then, in the summer, I was invited to Yorkshire to see those bright young things graduating from the army college and afterwards, we stopped off for tea in a hotel. As we walked into the dining room to be shown to our table, a sudden hush descended. Then, one by one, people rose to their feet and started clapping spontaneously. Tears were streaming down some of their faces as men, women and children cheered and called out my name.

For a moment, I didn't know what had happened. At first, I looked behind me to see if someone famous had arrived after us. 'What's all this about?' I asked Hannah, who was at my side. 'What are they doing that for?'

'They're delighted to see you,' my daughter said, grinning and waving at the crowd. 'They're showing their appreciation.'

'Appreciation for what?' I asked, confused.

'For giving them hope,' she said, placing a hand on my shoulder as all the cameras and phones came out and the cheering and clapping grew louder.

I was completely taken aback by this unashamed display of emotion and I have to admit that I became quite emotional myself. It was the first time anything like that had ever happened to me. My arrival somehow seemed to elevate the mood of the entire place. I didn't know how to react.

I thought that the next time it happened I would know what to expect, but none of it. When we were invited to a ceremony in Keighley town centre the police had to be summoned to control the traffic and the crowds. It reminded me of my childhood days at the town Gala with everyone gathering together, chatting and smiling as the flower-decked floats went by. The reaction in Keighley some ninety years on was an absolute hoot because if I'd dropped in there before all this happened, no one would have taken a blind bit of notice of an old man in a wheelchair. And there wouldn't have been the slightest chance of me being singled out for anything special at all.

Even when I went to hospital to have my hip checked recently, people walking past where I was seated stopped and did a double take before breaking out into the biggest smiles. And whenever I'm sitting at home in my lounge and there are workmen in the garden (as there very often are), I spot them peering sheepishly through the window on the off chance.

They want me to see them and smile, and then they smile back. It doesn't cost me owt and I get so much from seeing their expectant faces. In all the excitement there has been around my walk, I don't think many people know how much hope and inspiration I've enjoyed in return from their heart-warming reaction. It's been a two-way street.

How lucky I am to be in a position of being one to spread such joy and hope by something so simple as a smile or a little wave. It's been a rare and unexpected gift. I suppose that I'm the living proof that things will get better. They certainly did for me. I wouldn't have got through life if I didn't believe that. We have to remain hopeful that, whatever problems we are facing, we'll survive them and be a little happier tomorrow than we are today. This thought alone is enough to put some hope in our hearts for a better tomorrow, and that's good enough for me.

9.

Find Your Purpose

*'Whatever you want to do, you can
do it – if you want it badly enough.'*

Stirling Moss (1929–2020)

————————————

Last year I received a letter from a stranger, one
of thousands. What stood out about this par-
ticular note was that its author was in prison
for a serious crime, the details of which he didn't choose
to share. What he did confide was that he'd already
served several years and still had time to go, so I don't
think it was for a parking offence. In a way, I'm glad
I don't know.

'Dear Captain Tom,' he wrote.

*I've been following your fundraising and
I'm impressed by your stamina. Even though it*

doesn't look easy, you just keep going and are determined not to give up. You've proved what can be achieved with effort and the support of people around you. I never got on with my family, but I love seeing the way you are with yours, so I've decided to write to mine for the first time in years and hopefully we can move past all the bad stuff. If you can do something this hard, then I reckon I can too, so thanks for giving me a reason to go on.

His note moved me deeply and was one of those humbling consequences of my walk that appeared to give others purpose too. To learn that someone like that had been given the incentive to think again about what he'd done and change his attitude was both welcome and unexpected. I only hope that his family were receptive, and his wishes granted. It will give them all some reason to face the future. His wasn't the only such message, as I had hundreds of cards and letters from men, women and children all over the world who said they were inspired to find a new path for themselves because of me.

We all need a reason to get up in the morning and it's so important to have a purpose, or to find one for yourself. It takes courage, faith and optimism to try something new, but quite often all it needs is for something or someone to stir people up and make them think, 'I could do that,' or maybe at least try. My purpose that first Sunday in April 2020 when I started walking was solely to improve my mobility, but with a promised reward of £1 a lap it took on a new purpose: to raise a bit of money for those on the frontline. Both felt very important to me, and – with the encouragement of my family – I plodded on, never imagining what would happen.

I think it may have helped that I've always been quite driven and have enjoyed a clear sense of direction right back to my determination to be independent as a lad. There have undoubtedly been times in my life when I lost my way for a while, and there are plenty I've come across who suffered the same fate. If that happens and you can rediscover your purpose or set yourself a new goal, it will allow you to look forward instead of back. Even if it is simply to be kinder or more positive, do more exercise or reconnect with your youth, that will be the first step on the road to discovering a new lease of life. And only by doing so can you change your fortunes.

Everything in my past leads me to that conclusion, dating right back to Grandfather Thomas. He grew up in great poverty on a tenant farm near Hawes, the son of an agricultural labourer whose wife died when their children were small. Thomas's only prospect in life would have been to follow in his ancestor's footsteps, building stone walls or tending a few sheep for little reward.

I don't know what it was that gave him the courage to leave and move to Bradford to develop his building skills. If I could only go back and ask him about it, I would. Having set his course and learned his trade as a mason, Thomas married and found work building a wall around a vast new estate. It was the high quality of his workmanship on that job that led him to great fortune, until he became one of Keighley's most respected and beloved builders.

It was with reluctance that my deaf father ended up

inheriting the family building firm, but he did the best he could in the circumstances and found his own sense of purpose in photography; a hobby he also enthused me with. His passion for it gave him such pleasure because he appreciated the value of recording the inter-war years. Having unearthed many of his pictures recently, I was thrilled to pass them on to local historians to be preserved for all time. Looking through them for the first time in decades, I realized that the best lesson I learned from Father wasn't picked up in the darkroom but in his everyday life. He taught me to make the most of my situation and focus on something I liked, pursuing it so that I could do it to the best of my ability.

Purpose is a habit to encourage and develop from an early age, especially for members of the younger generation amongst whom there is a worrying rise in teenage depression. When I were a lad, there didn't seem to be time to feel down as there were always things to be getting on with. If you wanted something you had to set about trying to make it yourself or save up for it through hard work. If you needed to find out more about something, then you had to walk to the library with your satchel full of books and thumb through an encyclopaedia.

These days children don't have to move from the sofa; they can find all that they want with the click of a button. Nor do they need to memorize so much because they have it all at their fingertips. But irrespective of the source, it's learning and discovery that encourages creativity and ideas. And the inspiration for these can sometimes be found in some seemingly unlikely places.

There is a tendency these days not to fix anything any more but to simply buy a new version of whatever has broken, which wasn't always so. When I was about six my father gave me the best present of all – a block of wood, a hammer and some nails, so that I'd discover how to make something for myself. There were no teddy bears or traditional toys for this Keighley boy. Later on, he gave me a chunk of stone and a chisel and arranged for me to work alongside a stonemason, knowing that the skills I picked up would be useful in later life. I remember going at it hammer and tongs one day when the craftsman stopped me and told me to slow down. 'It took that stone a lifetime to get like that,' he said. 'You can't hurry these things.' He was right, you couldn't. They'd call it mindfulness today, but time spent focused on mending and making brings satisfaction and a peace of mind that goes hand in hand with learning a new skill.

Before I even reached my teens, I knew how to fix every kind of engine and could dismantle one piece by piece before putting it back together again in reverse order. On a long journey I'd carry oil and water for the radiator as well as tools and petrol, confident that I could solve any mechanical problem. Every day felt to have a purpose to it and everything that had a purpose was valued, not just chucked away.

In the 1970s, I'd often take my daughters to the council tip with our household waste because I wanted to teach them the value of things, and we'd generally return home with more than we dumped. We salvaged a discarded bicycle and a doll's pram that we repaired together, and one day we discovered an inflatable boat. I brought it home and spent several hours pumping it up and then covering it in soapy water to see where the (multiple) holes were. Once patched, it was taken straight to the beach where it provided months of fun.

It is not in my nature to stand idly by and let something perfectly good go to waste, but I'm probably out of date now because spanners and chisels, puncture patches and glue don't seem to be so important any more.

Finding your purpose even in small things is especially important as you get older because without that sense that you're busy and valuable to society or those around you, boredom can set in. In my life, the word boredom never existed. As I always told my children and grandchildren, 'If you can't find something to do then come to me and I'll give you something.' That pretty much guaranteed that they'd be busying themselves with something within minutes.

When you have purpose and drive – no matter what your age – you also become more fun and a far more interesting person to be around. This, in turn, creates positivity. A new hobby or a challenging repair job can become a topic of conversation or inspire others to try something similar. Planning an adventure or a road trip can take weeks and the excitement can be shared. Even something as simple as reading an interesting book or making a new dish can spark new conversations and help you through the most challenging periods of your life.

My wife Pamela had several girlfriends whose husbands were bored and unhappy in their retirement years without a sense of purpose. Often, the light in them went out altogether. There is a rising divorce rate in retired couples for this very reason, so it is imperative that you find something to keep your mind and body occupied.

The early years of my own retirement were some of the happiest of my life because Pamela and I immediately took on a whole new lease of life and relocated to southern Spain where we found all manner of things to fill our sunny days. There was a bit of work needed on our new house, so I got on with that and was kept fully occupied. When I wasn't doing DIY, we'd drive around in search of new experiences (or go shopping in Gibraltar so Pamela could buy a few essentials from Marks & Spencer). Friends and family would come and stay, and we had a dog that always enjoyed a long walk. I never regretted retiring or missed work. I still had a reason to get up every day. It was a very satisfying and happy time.

When we came back to Britain and Pamela became unwell and eventually went into a home, I decided that it was time for me to go back to work, even though I was approaching my nineties. I had my pension and savings, but I wanted to keep myself busy, so I scanned the newspapers and applied for several lower management jobs. 'Your age is against you, Mr Moore,' one of my prospective employers told me. 'Nonsense!' I protested. 'I bet you I can work harder than any of your staff.' In the end I was forced to accept that I was probably unemployable, and so I went back to my own busy world, content to be 'just' a pensioner keeping myself happily occupied, little knowing what lay around the corner.

Although I'm no longer walking for the NHS, the renewed sense of purpose that it gave me and came with everything that's followed has been invigorating. There's never been a dull moment. As everyone keeps reminding me, 'You can't die yet, Tom!' and it's true,

I'm far too busy and will have to shuffle off this mortal coil some other time that's more convenient. Besides, I'm not quite done. I want to keep going and trying to make a difference to people's lives by inspiring hope and positivity for as long as I can.

As Churchill once said, 'It is wonderful what great strides can be made when there is a resolute purpose behind them,' and you don't argue with Winston.

IO.

You'll Never Walk Alone

> *'Comradeship makes a man feel warm and courageous when all his instincts tend to make him cold and afraid.'*

Field Marshal Montgomery (1887–1976)

My wife Pamela and her best friend Janet were never happier than when they were out shopping together. Sometimes they'd meet up with other friends for lunch. When Pam got home, she'd unpack her bags, make some tea, and then pick up the telephone to call Janet before spending the next two hours chatting about their day. She was often so long on the phone that when she finished the call, she'd complain that her arm ached from holding the receiver to her ear.

I simply couldn't understand that. What on earth could there be to say? I couldn't talk for two hours about anything, least of all after I'd spent a whole day with that person. It was a complete mystery to me, but it happened so often I came to believe that women are much better at friendships than men. By contrast, I'd always been a bit of a loner who never sought the distraction of noise and chatter. I didn't once feel that I needed the company of a friend and, perhaps because I was so self-contained, no one was calling me up or knocking on my door day after day.

Although I'd had a handful of boyhood friends with whom to play kick-can or go walking and cycling with, I never actively sought them out. My immediate family was all I really needed.

When I joined the Army as a young man it was a whole new experience for me in so many ways. Chiefly, that I was suddenly thrown into the company of others; men with whom I lived in close proximity, day in, day out, with no chance of breaking away on my own. I quickly learned to make sacrifices and to compromise in order to fit in although, to my surprise, they quickly formed their own little cliques, something that was completely alien to me. Nevertheless, I was welcomed by all and made friends with lots of people, and we were able to work together as a team.

Two young lads called Jim and Philip became my closest pals and we supported each other throughout the war but without living in each other's pockets. That's when I began to appreciate the true value of camaraderie and came to understand that no man can go through life completely alone. There is enormous value in getting to know your comrades and to understand their characters, especially in times of conflict. I made good and lifelong friends this way and also learned the bitter-sweet sorrow of losing some of them along the way.

My wartime experience in the Far East served me well so that when I went into business after the war, I was able to work happily alongside colleagues and staff, understanding the importance of keeping up morale and rewarding a job well done. In the building trade I tried to be mindful of sensitivities about everything from racial tensions to pay and unions. Most of all, I wanted my people to learn how to work together in good faith and to know that I was someone who was approachable and open to suggestions, just as a few years earlier, my fellow soldiers had been. Teamwork was everything and we ended up creating a happy little community at the concrete factory.

As a busy working man with a family to care for, I didn't have much time for personal friends in my middle years, but I'd always enjoyed the company of those fellow military veterans with whom I'd made a unique bond and had kept in touch. The reunions I first instigated for the Duke of Wellington's regiment went on for sixty-five years, which might even qualify me for another Guinness World Record. Our annual gatherings were almost tribal as we caught up on each others' fortunes and renewed connections that had been forged in the heat of the jungle.

Although our members fell away one by one until I was the only man left standing, for all that time we bolstered each other through the wind and the rain. Each year when we met for our convivial catch-up, we'd privately note how others had aged, or how much thinner, frailer, or shrunken they looked. We watched as dementia crept into once brilliant minds, making rheumy-eyed soldiers quieter, or how arthritis and disease started to bend them double and make them doddery – me included.

Some of the men got themselves stuck in a rut, physically or emotionally, due to bereavement or a lack of purpose, illness or general unhappiness, and several stopped coming at all. Many had only two topics of conversation – the weather and their health – with fierce competition between them about who had suffered the most. Nevertheless, we supported each other as best we could, and our sense of comradeship only deepened. For those of us with a more positive outlook these nostalgic trips down memory lane were truly a force for good.

Sitting around the dinner table with a coffee or a glass of brandy, the last of the old crew shared stories of our various campaigns, or newer ones of grandchildren and family accomplishments. Wives and daughters started filling seats as our numbers dwindled and then some latter-day 'Dukes' joined in, eager to hear our tales. I attended so many funerals that name after name was crossed out in my address book, each one a colourful memory. The circle of comradeship that I'd enjoyed for so many years shrank away.

With none left who shared my history I had no one to reminisce with about my years in India and Burma or to confirm that it even happened. Nor was there anyone to confide in that the war was one of the best things that ever happened to me. I didn't ever expect to be in uniform, but it was the right thing to do and – once I was – I worked hard and made the most of it, rising from private to captain in short order.

In fact, when I look back, I realize that my whole life pivoted on that war, because if I hadn't been drafted I'd have stayed on at college and become a civil engineer. I suspect I'd have carried on being a rather self-contained and isolated person, because I might never have known the true value of friendship and the benefit of mutual support, nor of the rewards born of engaging with strangers from all walks of life.

Happily, the sense of military brotherhood is still there with the new friends I've made via the Dukes; men and women who served more recently than I, and who've proved loyal companions. We keep in touch largely by mail and telephone as I answer questions about different events and battles the regiment went through, some of which only I can now answer.

It is a fact of life that those who survive the longest will outlive the rest. None of my contemporaries from Keighley remain either, so there's no one left that I can talk to at my level about the things I'd like to reminisce about, such as trams or Zeppelins, parkin, woollen swimwear, weekly baths or gaslights.

I've made some lovely new Yorkshire contacts recently; people who remind me what it was like to talk to my father and uncle because they have the self-same accents, which is a joy. But everyone else I grew up with has gone. As have all those men who marched into war with me. That's just how life goes. It doesn't cause me any concern; it just makes me a little sad.

When I think about my life during the last two decades, I realize that – just as had been the case when I was a boy – the only people still marching by my side are my immediate relatives. Moving in with my daughter Hannah and her family after Pamela died wasn't a decision I took lightly, not least because I'd just done up my house in Gravesend and fully expected it to be my last residence on this earth. Part of me didn't want to move at all but, at eighty-six, I was persuaded that I shouldn't be living alone.

If I'd stayed on my own ninety miles away in Kent, I would have been perfectly capable and competent – until the day I fell. And in lockdown, I'd have had to rely on the kindness of strangers, so it would have been different and rather lonely, I suspect. Instead, I discovered the immeasurable value in having the support of the family who never expected anything less of me than to get better and get on with my life. They knew I'd not given up before and that I wasn't going to start now. Under their watchful gaze, I reached inside myself in those darkest of days and found the strength to carry on.

This unexpected blessing is never brought home to me more than when I think of the homeless or the disenfranchised; those who are totally alone with nobody to help or protect them. That was surely never the intention when they were born. There are plenty of others who are completely isolated because of disability, poverty or mental health, with little human contact or chance of reconciliation with their families. Like the prisoner who wrote to me, especially if things don't work out for him. That's why it is so important that we look after one another from the beginning to the end.

Thankfully, both at home and across this wonderful country of ours, I feel surrounded by people encouraging me to take another step and another then another. Each step starts where the other finishes and leads to the next. And it is all the more special if you have someone beside you to catch you if you fall.

Epilogue

> *'That is the great fallacy, the wisdom of old men. They do not grow wise. They grow careful.'*

Ernest Hemingway (1899–1961)

---

*E*very night when I go to bed, I perform all my morning tasks in reverse order before saying a little prayer and sliding under the duvet. Closing my eyes, I assess how my body feels after a day of activity, holding my head in my hands and allowing my gnarled fingers to follow the contours of my skull. The thought occurs to me that this lump of bone is 100 years old, something I'd never considered before. If it was a vase or a bowl, it might even be valuable.

Being this old probably explains why my hearing has diminished over the years. After all, I am listening *through century-old ears. Without my aids, I'm plunged into a world of silence much like my father's. I've had two new knees to stop them complaining, but I lost my teeth a long time ago, probably due to my childhood habit of crunching sugar lumps.*

Having always been five feet ten inches, I have shrunk quite a bit in recent years, curled over as I am like a human question mark. This has changed my shape so that I now need to tighten my belt to stop my trousers falling down.

Two things I haven't lost yet are my sight and my marbles. I've worn glasses for many a year and can still see perfectly well through them, which is a blessing – although when I look in the mirror these days I barely recognize the face staring back at me. As for my mind, well it gets a bit forgetful sometimes, but people assure me that I'm still sharp for my age.

Being so dreadfully old, I expected some physical limitations along with the normal deterioration of my bodywork, but I didn't bank on being quite so tired. This is something the younger generation doesn't always allow for. I am constantly surprised by how even the slightest exertion requires a nap or three to compensate.

There is nevertheless something almost reassuring about accepting the decline that I cannot prevent. A kind of calmness overcomes you when you realize that the end might come at any time. Death becomes somehow easier to think about and not something to be afraid of. It's not that I'm giving up; it's more a case of throttling back and quietly cruising along towards the inevitable. Just like when my eighty-five-year-old father gently told my sister, 'This will be my last meal,' before taking to his bed, never to rise again.

There are nights when I lie in my bed and wonder if I'll ever get up again, as I never thought I'd live this long. Nobody imagines being 100 and most of us believe we'll have done all right if we last as long as our parents did. Logic and science tell me that I shan't be around for many more years, but my competitive streak keeps me going.

None of us know when our time will come, but knowing that it will likely be sooner rather than later does focus the mind and makes every day precious.

People say we should live each day as if it's our last, but we can't be happy all the time. That would be bad for us. Life isn't perfect and we have to feel sorrow sometimes to know what happiness is. But we can at least choose to find some joy in each and every day.

My advice would be not to assume that you'll live as long as me and don't put anything really important off, because tomorrow could be your last. Forgiveness is a good place to start because it isn't healthy to keep carrying bitterness in your heart. Nobody is perfect. Accept that and move on. There's not enough time in this life to waste it on anger and hatred.

People often ask me what the secret to old age is, but I really don't have one other than to keep breathing. I've never paid much attention to health advice and have eaten whatever I liked. The good news is that when you get to my age everyone treats you with kindness and respect. You can't put a foot wrong because no one dares argue with you.

I am also often asked if I have a 'bucket list', and although there are a few places I have said I might hope to visit, I've done almost all that I want to do and, in any event, I'm afraid to mention anything in case it gets arranged. On one TV appearance I said it would be fun to travel across America on Route 66 – riding my motorbike. I'm not sure I'm up to all that time on a motorbike now, so I joked that I'd settle for a Bentley. But I should be careful what I wish for because the next thing I knew, someone offered to provide me with a luxury car!

I must admit that I do miss gadding about, but I doubt I'll have time to do much more. This old chassis has had a good run and is soon headed for the scrapheap. Not that there'll be much to salvage, mind. I find myself wondering what the end will be like and whether I've had my last bowl of porridge.

I only pray that I don't linger on or go into a home. That would be a final mercy. Once that happens, I want everyone to say, 'Well done, Tom!' and hopefully reflect that I've done a bit of good. Life will go on. Babies will be born. People will eventually forget about Captain Tom. For a while, though, I'll be remembered for the last few years of my life rather than those that went before, and that's a rare blessing in a world that tends to celebrate youthful endeavour.

Previously, my funeral would have made one little line in the local newspaper and been attended by only a handful of people, but I expect there'll be a few more now. Someone will have to make extra cake and sandwiches, and it won't be me. I want the service to end with 'My Way' by Frank Sinatra because I always did things my way and especially like the line about having too few regrets to mention.

It's odd and rather touching to think that people might weep over my passing – strangers I've never even met. If I can, I'd like to watch my own funeral from a distance. That would be quite the joke as I looked down and chuckled at everyone making a lot of fuss over me.

Even though I have a space reserved in the village churchyard, I want to be cremated and my ashes taken back to Yorkshire to be with my parents and grandparents in the Moore family plot. I wouldn't mind having a little white headstone somewhere to mark my existence, a bit like the ones they have in military cemeteries. Nothing too fancy.

Several people have asked me what my epitaph might be, so I've given that a bit of thought too. When I was younger, I enjoyed listening to The Goon Show *on the wireless, and one of the comedians who always made me laugh the hardest was Spike Milligan. Like me, he fought in the Second World War, but was wounded in Italy. When he died at the age of eighty-three, he wrote his own epitaph, which was engraved in Gaelic on his headstone. It reads: 'I told you I was ill.'*

This always made me laugh, so I think I'd ask for the simple inscription of my name, the dates of my earthly span, and the words: 'I told you I was old.'

That'll do me. And hopefully, some day it will make someone smile.